TRUCKS IN BRITAIN

ROUNDOAK PUBLISHING

First published in 1995 by
Roundoak Publishing
Nynehead, Wellington, Somerset, England TA21 0BX

© Copyright 1995 POVC & Roundoak Publishing

ISBN 1 871565 22 7 – Softback   ISBN 1 871565 23 5 – Hardback

Design and Typesetting by Character Graphics, Taunton
Printed in England by Amadeus Press, Huddersfield

Front cover: The bonnetted Morris Y was superseded by the flat-fronted
Morris J in 1951 and these vans were bought as 100cf. mailvans for the
following ten years. One of the later Morris JBs, a 1961 van, is pictured in
Battersea in the spring of 1966. (D.J.Foster)

Back cover – top: Sherpa postbus L48 GOK operates a twice-daily postbus
service from Leek in Staffordshire to Hartington in Derbyshire. It is seen at
the boundary stone of the Peak National Park near Onecote. This particular
service was introduced in 1994 and illustrates the expansion of postbus
services away from the traditional locations of Scotland and Wales. Besides
passenger-carrying duties, it also operates on mailvan duties in Stoke-on-
Trent. (M.W.Skillen)

Back cover – bottom: This 1956 Morris Commercial LCS 240cf. mailvan
operated at St Albans until disposal, but was repurchased by the Post Office
and restored to original condition – it was moved from Basildon to the new
Dunton workshop where it was photographed in February 1995. (D.A.Cott)

This page: This 105cf. mailvan was based on the Morris-Commercial 15cwt.
chassis. 142 were purchased in 1932 and YY 1910 was photographed in the
picturesque location of St. Mawes in Cornwall. (GPO)

Contents

Introduction

A photographic history of the Royal Mail fleet is inevitably dominated by smaller vehicles - the familiar 'Little red van' that can be found the length and breadth of the United Kingdom, collecting from remote letter boxes and delivering to isolated cottages. The Morris Minor has a special place in the history of Royal Mail and in the hearts of both enthusiasts and the general public – everyone's favourite mailvan and restored examples attract attention whenever they appear. But look again, there is much more to the Royal Mail fleet – from postbuses linking rural communities with the outside world, to heavyweight artics linking our major cities – the Royal Mail operates one of the largest and most efficient commercial fleets in Britain, and has for many years exercised a powerful influence on the development of road transport.

The Post Office has its origins in the private courier network of the monarch, consisting of messengers on horseback stationed at 'posts' at regular intervals on the roads radiating from London. In 1635, King Charles opened the network to the public, and an Act of Parliament in 1656 established a formal postal system. The first stage coaches ran in 1658 but were restricted by the poor state of the roads and the narrow streets in towns. The roads and the coaches developed during the eighteenth century – John Besant of London built the 'Patent Coach', and his work was continued into the nineteenth century by John Vidler and his sons at the Millbank coach works, where coaches were cleaned and serviced each morning for their outward journeys – in effect, the first Post Office Road Transport workshops. Mail coaches operated twenty-three radial routes out of London, departing every evening, transferring mail en-route to cross-post mail coaches, mounted riders and foot messengers for onward transmission. Horses and carts were used in London to transfer the mail between the various inns and coffee houses where the coaches terminated. Due to the high cost of postage the mail was mostly for business customers, but when the uniform penny post was introduced in 1840, a rapid expansion occurred, and mail was transferred onto the developing railways.

Mail transport was provided by private contractors, some of whom were quick to experiment with motor transport, the first being introduced in October 1897 at the same time as the introduction of daily delivery of letters, leading to the first purchase by the General Post Office (GPO) of bicycles. In 1903, the provision of Post Office cycles became a Stores Department function, and a Stores Transport Department was established, headed by Major C. Wheeler, OBE. The first vehicle to be used by the GPO was a Wallis and Steevens traction engine for stores use in 1905, followed by a Alldays & Onions car for the Sectional Engineer at Gloucester in 1906, and a Maudslay petrol lorry (Stores No. 1) in 1907. Mail transport, however, was still mainly carried out by contractors using both horse-drawn and motorised transport, although by 1909 more than five thousand postmen were using bicycles and carrier- tricycles to Major Wheeler's specification. Pedal cycles were not popular in hilly terrain and in 1914 the Engineer-in-Chief requested Treasury approval for the purchase of four motor cycle combinations for use in districts which were ill-provided with facilities for locomotion.

After the war, the GPO experimented with ex-War Department Fords and this was followed by the purchase of the first new mailvans in 1920. The use of mailvans expanded considerably during the 1920s and 1930s, initially using Ford vans and BSA motor cycle combination and later Morris or Morris-Commercial vans.

In the early days, the GPO was organised as a centralised structure with most of the management authority in London. Royal Mail was structured into 17 Districts (London, North Eastern, Scottish, South Eastern, South Western, Western, South Wales, North Wales, Eastern, North Midland, South Midland, Birmingham, Manchester, Bristol, Belfast, Liverpool and North Western) with very limited autonomy and with 450 local Head Postmasters. It was these local Head Postmasters whose titles were carried on the nearside of mailvans up to the reorganisation of 1986. The late 1930s saw the districts being replaced with nine larger regions with much greater autonomy. By January 1968, the number of Head Postmasters had reduced to 398 and this number reduced sharply to 183 by early 1970 as the smaller offices were merged into larger units to give savings in administration costs.

In October 1969, the General Post Office became the Post Office Corporation. Vehicle registration, which had been centralised in London from the early 1920s was immediately devolved to local Head Postmasters which resulted in registrations appropriate to the locality rather than from London.

1981 saw the telephone service of the Post Office being formed into a separate company known as British Telecommunications and five years later the Post Office reorganised its remaining operations into three separate businesses – Letters, Parcels and Counters. Each has gone their separate ways and each now has a distinct identity. The Parcels service launched itself as Parcelforce in 1989, the Letters business adopted a higher profile identity in 1990 with a new logo and Counters increasingly markets itself as THE POST OFFICE. Royal Mail reorganised again in 1992 and is now based around nine Divisional organisations.

Royal Mail's vehicles have carried fleet numbers (known as serials) from the earliest days of motor vehicle operation. A progressive numbering system was initially adopted, starting at 1 which extended to 1457 in 1935 but this included Post Office Stores vehicles as well as mailvans. In 1935 the series reverted to 001 but Morris vehicles were separately numbered in a series 2000 onwards from 1926. These two series reached 0999 (then jumped to 1501– 1999) and 5999 respectively. Subsequent series were 10000-15999, 20000-25999, 30000-35999, 40000-45999, 50000-56301, 60000-65999, 71000-75999, 90000-94999, 100000-105978, 220800-230795. 269800-276759 with the missing numbers generally allocated to telephone vehicles. Other types had their own serial numbers, motor cycle combinations were numbered M1-M21, then a series 1 to 2933, telegram motor cycles were numbered in a series from T1 which reached T5999 in 1962, then moved to T14000-T15963 and then T280800-T283484. In 1971, the system was completely revised and vehicles now carry a seven-figure serial number made up of the final year of purchase, two numbers denoting type and four numbers identifying the individual vehicle from 0001 upwards. Parcelforce vehicles from 1987 have been numbered separately in sequences from 5001 upwards.

Much of the interest in Royal Mail stems from the use of the cypher on the vehicles. Vehicles have carried George, Edward and Elizabeth although vehicles in Scotland have carried the King's cypher during the present monarch's reign to give further variety. The 1953 livery was the first where the letters ROYAL MAIL were rendered in gold and this style lasted until 1975. The 1975 livery continued with the Royal Cypher but used modernised lettering for the 'Royal Mail' in a contemporary double- line style. This logo lasted until 1990 when a bolder lettering style with yellow stripes emphasised the separate image of Royal Mail as part of the Post Office.

Throughout this book vehicles are referred to by their capacity in cubic feet (cf.) and this reflects the official classification to capacity rather than weight by Royal Mail over the years. The size of the smallest van has progressively increased from 30cf. in 1932, through 35cf., 50cf. in 1940 to 80cf. from the early 1980s. The largest size of vehicle in use today is the 40 foot tri-axle semi-trailer, which is rated at 2250cf.

It is fortunate that many vehicles from the earlier years were photographed by the GPO and that these views have survived to the present day to give such a comprehensive selection to illustrate the GPO fleet. We are grateful to Royal Mail Road Transport for permitting the use of many official GPO photographs in this book. Most of the remaining photographs are from the cameras of members of the Post Office Vehicle Club, an enthusiast group dedicated to the study of all aspects of postal and telecommunications vehicles.

The Early Years

The Stores Dept. of the General Post Office was the first to experiment with mechanised transport and hired a Wallis & Stevens traction engine for four weeks in 1904. In 1905, a similar second-hand, but unregistered, machine was bought for £450 and a Maudslay lorry was bought in January 1907 for £727 – both for the Stores Dept. Meanwhile the engineering fleet had obtained a car at Gloucester in 1906.

The first trials with Royal Mail of motorised transport, twenty postal Motor Cycle Combinations, with a capacity of 18cf., were placed into service in 1914 to replace postmen on horseback. They comprised four Rovers, ten New Hudsons and 6 Douglas machines. They were all single-cylinder machines of 3½hp with wicker or metal side-carriers. A further Rover Motor Cycle Combination, this time of 14cf., joined the postal fleet in 1915 as a reserve, together with four Tricars of 6hp. – two each by Autocarrier and Warwick.

Difficulties with contractors immediately after World War I led to trials at Eastbourne with two ex W.D light Fords fitted with bodies of approximately 75cf. capacity, followed by the purchase of a second-hand GWK light van for use at Kingston-on-Thames in February 1920. Trials of the three postal vans were so successful that the GPO requested Treasury approval for the purchase of fifty new GWK 8cwt. light vans of 80cf. capacity to replace contractors in rural localities. These vehicles were delivered between June and October 1920 and they were shortly followed by a further five but the make was to prove a disappointment and considerable difficulties were experienced with their drive train and they were quickly replaced by Fords.

More postal Motor Cycle Combinations entered service in 1920, this time larger two-cylinder machines with carriers of 24-32cf. capacity. A further 100 GWK mailvans were supplied in 1921/22 followed by 200 Fords, including 40 light vans and 10 one-tonners and a special 30cwt. chassis which was extended by Baico to accommodate a body of 320cf. capacity. Purchases for Royal Mail in 1922/23 included 87 Ford 105cfs., 2 Ford Baico 320 cfs., a single GWK (the last) and some motor cycles.

The GPO was under considerable pressure to buy British and 1924 saw two Morris 105cf. prototypes purchased and the make gradually displaced the American-manufactured Ford which was assembled at Trafford Park in Manchester. A few Trojans were bought as well but the Morris- Commercial chassis soon became the standard mailvan for the GPO.

Right: The Post Office has been moving mails for over 350 years and the original means of transport was the stage or mail coach that had a mail compartment as well as carrying a guard. The coaches criss-crossed the country carrying mail between the major centres. This particular print is of the Glasgow to London mail coach. (GPO)

Above: Once the mail reached a major destination 'cross posts' would carry it on to its ultimate destination. Small carts would be used for this purpose and they would also deliver items to the outlying parts of the district served by the sorting office. This photograph taken at Wangford in Suffolk around 1905 clearly shows the secure wicker basket. (GPO)

Left: After the introduction of the 'penny post' in 1840 the volume of mail requiring transport increased to the extent that mail coaches could not cope. The railway revolution was under way and mail would be transported by train although the GPO also continued to used road contractors for certain long-distance journeys. Horse-drawn carts would be used to get the mail to the railway station and this Christmas view shows a hired cart in the foreground with a more usual horse-drawn cart in the background with a poster extorting the public to Post Early for Christmas. (GPO)

Below left: As they do today, parcels required special vehicles and this is a fine example of the type used at the time. The location is Edinburgh. The 'Royal Parcels Mail' lettering was readopted by the Post Office in the mid-1980s in a slightly different format. (GPO)

Opposite top left: Thought to be the first motorised vehicle used for mail delivery contracts in Scotland and operated by Stirling's Motor Carriage Co. of Glasgow. It was used for a service between Inverary and Ardrishaig from June 1898 and covered the 26 miles in 3 hours and 7 minutes. The vehicle continued to be used on the service until the winter of 1898/99 when bad road conditions and mechanical failures led to reversion to horses. Motor vehicles were not used on the service again until May 1910 when an Arrol-Johnston car was tried. Permanent motor operation commenced in May 1914. (GPO)

Opposite: This is an 1899 Daimler Motor Co. parcels van, it had a vertical twin petrol engine, tube ignition, three-speed transmission and chain drive. (GPO)

ROYAL MAIL

Above: Smaller quantities of parcels were delivered by tricycle and this early example shows the wooden and canvas container. The Carrier was made by Singer & Co. of London & Coventry. Note the ornate cypher of Queen Victoria carried predominately on the front of the parcels container. (GPO)

Above: Thomas Tilling Limited of London and Brighton had extensive contracts with the GPO in the London area, and operated the London to Brighton route using three Milnes-Daimler vans – this one being photographed outside Brighton Head Post Office in 1905. (GPO)

Left: Another large contractor was McNamara of Castle Street, Finsbury, north London and it continued to provide transport for the Royal Mail until after the Second World War. This Dennis dates from about 1914 and a replica of this vehicle was built by the Post Office at Kidbrooke for the Lord Mayor's Show of November 1970 based on a BMC 250JU chassis. (GPO)

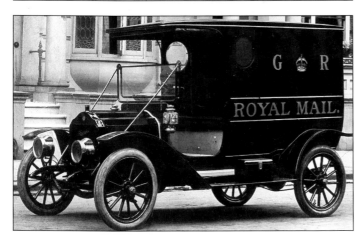

Left: One of the earliest Studebaker vans – based on its car design and built in Indiana, USA – was operated on contract to the GPO. The photograph is dated 1913. (GPO)

ROYAL MAIL

Above: Possibly an early Renault van, the vehicle being photographed outside the Head Post Office in Bristol. Note the spare tyre and the elaborate horn. (GPO)

Right: In 1914, twenty Motor Cycle Combinations, with a capacity of 18cf., were introduced to replace postmen on horseback. They comprised of four Rover, ten New Hudson and six Douglas machines. They were all single cylinder of 3½hp with wicker or metal side carriers. This is one of the four Rovers which operated at Helensburgh, Slough and Alnwick.

Left: One of four 6hp tricars, supplied by Warwick and Autocarrier in 1915, photographed outside Oakham Head Post Office – this one is of Warwick of Reading manufacture. Its purchase price is recorded as being 100 guineas. (GPO)

Left: After the GWKs, the GPO purchased 625 Fords between 1921 and 1925. Some, certainly those purchased in 1921 and 1922, were reconditioned ex War Department chassis. This one is XL 770, a one-tonner with Bonallack & Sons. Ltd. 250cf. bodywork and serial number 251, new in 1922. (GPO)

Right: The American-built Ford converted in Britain by Baico with a longer chassis and chain-drive was bought by the GPO in small numbers. The 320cf. body was very unusual in having a sliding side door. (GPO)

Below right: In 1923 two electric tractors were purchased for moving mail between sorting offices and railway stations. This is XR 2752 and the photograph was taken at Chester station in 1934. Note the duplicate registration plate on the battery box, it was provided for attachment to the rearmost trailer when on public roads. (GPO)

Opposite top: Also purchased in June 1920 was this second-hand left-hand drive Ford 1-ton van which was fitted with a high-sided body of 300cf. capacity. It was operated in Cheltenham, where it survived until 1924. (GPO)

Opposite bottom: The first GPO-owned mailvans were three second-hand vehicles, two Fords and a GWK. A further fifty GWKs were purchased in 1920 and this view shows three of the type parked together, probably in the London area as it is believed the GWKs were registered locally by each Head Postmaster rather than centrally in London. A further 106 GWKs followed the initial batch in 1920-1922 but the GPO had considerable difficulties with the drive train and the last of the 157 GWKs had been withdrawn by the end of 1925. (GPO)

Above: In addition to Ford one-tonners, 7/8 cwt. chassis were fitted with 105cf. bodies of the type illustrated by serial number 361. It was located at Cambridge and one of 42 similar vehicles bought in 1923. (GPO)

Left: The GPO bought ten Trojans with 70cf. bodywork as a trial against the Morris and Ford chassis in 1924/5. They had a four-cylinder 2-stroke engine, mounted under the cab floor and were chain-driven on one wheel only. The bonnet contained only the radiator, petrol tank and steering gear. (GPO)

Pre-War Expansion

The first production Morrises (six 70cfs., seven 105cfs, an 140cf. and five 250cfs.) arrived in 1925 and the chassis rapidly became the choice for all Royal Mail vans. They were equipped with a range of GPO-designed coachbuilt bodies built by a number of different bodybuilders but all to the same elegant design. The standard sizes of vans were 70, 105, 160, 250 and 340 cubic feet capacity, and each increment had only subtle changes in their dimensions to create a fleet of vehicles of similar appearance. Fords continued to be purchased in reducing numbers from 1926 to 1930 but thereafter Morris obtained all the orders for mailvans.

Also bought in 1925 were the first eleven solo motor cycles to complement the larger motor cycle combination that had motorised many rural delivery routes. Their use was not extended greatly and it decided in 1928 to standardise on a lighter motor cycle combination based on the same BSA 2hp four stroke model with a sidecar capacity of 8cf. – about 64 solos were converted to combinations in the 1928-1931 period. Solo motor cycles were not used for telegraph delivery until January 1933 but their use was then rapidly extended with 565 solo motor cycles purchased by the end of the decade for such work.

The Royal Mail fleet expanded very rapidly in this period; from a fleet of 810 vehicles in 1926 it grew to 4,399 vehicles in April 1933 and continued to grow to the outbreak of the war in 1939.

Of all the vehicles produced by Morris, the pre-war Minor played the most important part in the motorisation of the mails. A 5 cwt. van based on the contemporary overhead valve engined car was introduced in late 1929, but the GPO did not buy the model until 1932, by which time a side valve 847cc engine was standard. Bodywork was built to GPO design by a number of coachbuilders such as Duple, Bonallack and Park Royal, including many special features. In late 1934 the Minor was superseded by a van version of the Morris Eight car, but this was not adopted by the GPO, instead a hybrid was developed using the Minor chassis but

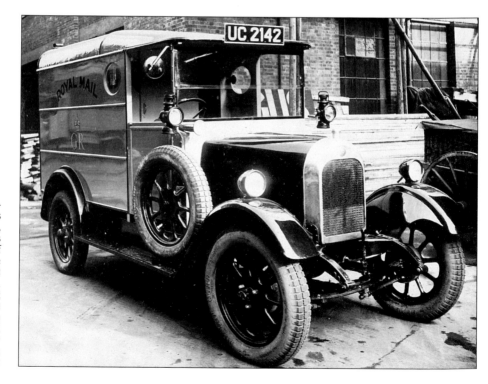

Right: In 1927/28 Morris-Commercial chassis dominated the orders, taking over from Ford as the favoured type of vehicle. 417 were purchased and UC 2142 was one of 179 70cf. examples. Note the front registration plate above the windscreen, a feature of pre-war mailvans and the simplified cypher introduced at about this time. (GPO)

many components from the Eight, including the 918cc side-valve engine, and later easiclean wheels in place of the wire ones. The hybrids remained in production for both mail and telephone use until early 1940 when the van version of the series E saloon, the series Z was introduced.

The arrival of the Morris Minor highlighted problems with the lightweight motor cycle combinations whose capacity of 8cf. was often inadequate and the lids of the sidecar had to be left insecure because of the loads being delivered; also their riders looked enviously at the comfort of the Morris Minor, particularly on exposed or arduous rural routes. The numbers of combinations reached 1,293 in October 1936 but thereafter reduced rapidly as combinations were replaced by Morris Minors - the small mailvan had become the backbone of the Royal Mail fleet.

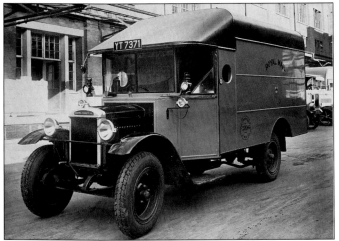

Above: Forty two 1-ton 250cf. Morris-Commercials entered service in 1927/28, this being YU 1431 based at Paddington. Also in the photograph is one of the many Motor Cycle Combinations. By this year some 231 examples of many differing makes had entered service. (GPO)

Left: The largest body size was the 340cf. based on the Morris-Commercial 25/30cwt. chassis. Also bought in 1927/28 were sixteen Morris Commercial 25/30cwt 340cf. vehicles. This is YT 7371 one of the 30cwt versions; its allocation roundel (a feature of mailvans to 1975) shows that it had serial number 2208 and was based at South Western District Office in London. It was registered in September 1927 and remained in service until April 1936. (GPO)

Left: 1928/29 saw experiments with electric vehicles and YX 7649 was one of three Electromobile 1-ton vehicles built on chassis imported from the USA. These were used at Leeds until about 1935. (GPO)

Right: YX 8253 was the second of seven Victor Electric model A 15cwt. mailvans purchased in May 1928 for trials at Mount Pleasant in London. They had a radius of operation of 20 miles per charge and a speed of 15 mph on the level but they gave unsatisfactory service and their running costs were $2^{1}/_{2}$ times those of contemporary mailvans. (GPO)

Left: In 1926 the first order was placed for twelve BSA $2^{3}/_{4}$hp 349cc Motor Cycle Combinations, they being known as Light Weight Combinations by the GPO to distinguish them from the larger Heavy Weight Combinations. The first six had sidecars of $6^{1}/_{4}$ cf. but thereafter 8cf. sidecars were specified. Early in 1928 it was decided to standardise on LWCs and 134 were delivered in 1928/29 including XV 4590, new in February 1929. This view shows clearly the 8cf. capacity lidded container, fitted with a Carbon Tetrachloride fire extinguisher that would not be permitted these days. (GPO)

Right: Also purchased in the same year were 71 solo machines. Like the previous photograph this is a BSA 2³/₄hp machine, and they were also used for letter deliveries initially but their use was extended to telegrams from 1933. The mail was carried in the panniers fitted on each side. (GPO)

Left: Motor Cycle Combinations continued to find favour in 1929/30 as a further 231 were purchased. At the same time 37 existing solos were converted to Combinations. BSA 2³/₄hp models were again specified. By now all the side carriers were of metal construction. (GPO)

Right: Three solo BSAs outside what appears to be the London Chief Office in King Edward Street. GU 7372 is a 2³/₄hp dating from 1929/30 while GH 1822 is a BSA YA 3¹/₂hp version. (GPO)

Above: A busy scene in King Edward Building sorting office yard in 1931 with mainly McNamara-owned Morris Commercial mailvans present. In the centre of the photograph by the lamp standard is the rear view of a Morris Commercial C 30cwt 340cf. registration GC 8274, introduced in 1929 and which differed considerably from the McNamara design. McNamara continued to provide contracts to the GPO until at least May 1948 when a batch of thirty Morris-Commercials registered HGF 66 to HGF 95 were purchased by the GPO. (GPO)

Left: A view of a full garage at Glasgow Post Office in the early 1930's. Most identifiable vehicles are of Morris Commercial manufacture in the 12cwt or 1-ton version with 105cf. and 250cf. capacity respectively – note the parking numbers hanging over the bays. (GPO)

Left: 107 Morris 12cwt. 105cf. vehicles were bought in 1930. GK 3235 (serial number 3552) was allocated to Edinburgh and is seen here making a delivery to Holyrood House in 1934. The side advertboard was a feature of mailvans until quite recently. (GPO)

Left: The first air mails were carried in 1911 and were flown from Heston to Windsor to celebrate the coronation of King George V. The Royal Air Mail Service first began operations in June 1930 and there were regular air mail services world-wide with three vans painted in a special blue livery and carrying air mail signs. This is a Morris 10cwt 70cf. vehicle new in May 1930, photographed at the Customs office at Croydon Aerodrome in 1933; it lasted until June 1937. (GPO)

Below: Fords continued to be bought up to 1930 and one of the last deliveries was of eight Model AA 30cwt. vehicles with 250cf. bodywork. (GPO)

Left: In 1931 twelve Morris Minor 30cfs. were purchased. Their capacity was reclassified the following year to 35cf. and they quickly became the most numerous vehicle in the Royal Mail fleet. This particular example, GW 6059, was allocated to Bedford; note the special small version of cypher produced for these vehicles. (GPO)

Below: Morris vehicles continued to flood into the fleet with a further 508 being purchased in 1932. Included in this total were 240 Morris 10cwt 70cf. vehicles of which YY 154 is an example, seen by Loch Lomond in 1934. New in September 1932, it remained in service until June 1939. (GPO)

Above: The Post Office has always had a network of motor transport workshops to maintain its vehicles, indeed at one time the policy was that a workshop would be established where a minimum of six vehicles were based, a far cry from today's policy which has seen many workshops being made redundant with the greater reliability and reduced servicing need of modern vehicles. Here a Morris C 15cwt 105cf. vehicle is hoisted to enable work to be carried out. (GPO)

Right: Another workshop scene showing repairs being carried to the rear çdoor of a Morris 15cwt 105cf. van. Note the improvised step enabling the mechanic to reach the door. No doubt the modern day factory inspector would have something to say about working practices. (GPO)

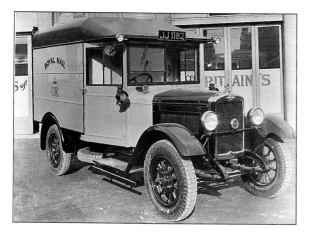
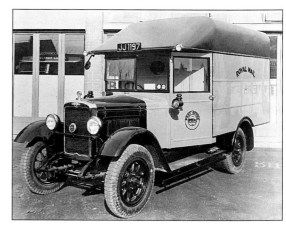

Above left & right: The GPO used a variety of coachbuilders for vehicle bodywork. Here Morris-Commercial 1-tonners are posed outside the Duple factory awaiting delivery in 1932. JJ 1182 is a 160cf. and JJ 1197 is a 250cf. (GPO)

Left: A Pashley wicker-basket tricycle from the 1930s found as a box of bits and fully restored to original condition, including building a reproduction basket, by its owner Dave Elder of Horsham (M.W.Skillen)

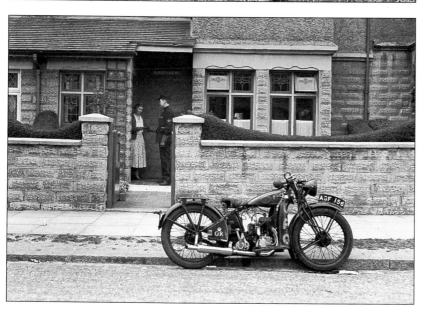

Left: In 1933 with the advent of three letter registrations, a different system was introduced. Instead of small batches of registrations, the L.C.C. allocated blocks to the GPO, initially of two hundred registrations but this was to prove inadequate and finally culminated in the allocation of a complete registration series, a practice that was to continue for 33 years from 1936 to 1969. AGF 156, a BSA 2.49hp solo motor cycle used for telegraph-delivery, is an example from the first three-letter registration block supplied to the GPO. (GPO)

Right: In April 1933, the Royal Mail fleet consisted of 4,399 vehicles of which no less than 2,673 were of Morris-Commercial manufacture. A further 622 Morrises were bought during 1933 of which ALR 639 is a 30cwt. 340cf. version. (GPO)

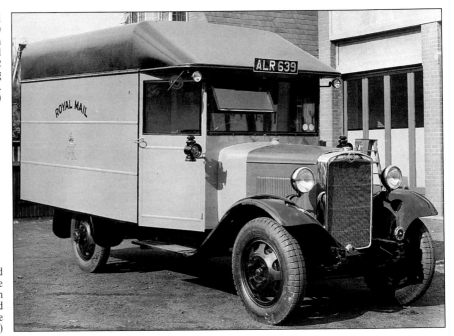

Below: Small vans could be found all over the country serving the furthest areas as can be seen from this example of a Penzance based Morris 10cwt 70cf. van at The Land's End Hotel in 1935. (GPO)

Right: Motor cycle combinations were the next most numerous vehicle in the postal fleet in 1933 with some 1202 being in service. By 1934 a further 325 had been introduced and AXL 938 is a BSA 4.99hp machine. Motor cycle combinations fell out of favour in the late 1930s as the volume of mail had grown to such an extent on many deliveries that the sidecar lid could no longer be secured on departure from the sorting office, and Morris Minors took over this work, particularly in rural areas with exposed or arduous routes. (GPO)

Left: The Morris Eight van was introduced in 1934 and evidently demonstrated to the GPO as illustrated here. No orders were forthcoming as the GPO preferred the established Morris Minor with coachbuilt bodywork; instead a special hybrid version of the Minor was built for both mail and telephone work. (GPO)

Below: A special airmail van was purchased in 1934 based on the Morris-Commercial L2/8 chassis with Duple streamlined bodywork and finished in the blue Royal Air Mail Service livery. It was used to inaugurate the Empire Air Mail Service at Croydon Aerodrome on 11th November 1934 and it was then used as a publicity vehicle for the Air Mail Service throughout the country. The design was commissioned by the GPO from Maurice Lambert, a contemporary designer and was the first break with tradition for the conservative General Post Office. (GPO)

Left: This view of BUU 142, a Morris 1-ton 160cf. clearly shows the locking bar traditionally fitted to all postal vans, a feature that continued to be specified until 1971. The bar was released from inside the cab of the vehicle. Note also the rear mounted tail lamp and the folding step. (GPO)

Below: A fine photograph of BXC 285 showing plenty of detail and the allocation to Taunton. It is a Morris-Commercial 15cwt 105cf. vehicle. (GPO)

Right and below: For publicity reasons the Ministry of Transport was approached with the request that the registration letters GPO should be allotted to the General Post Office for use on special publicity vehicles. The numbers GPO 1 and GPO 2 were allocated to two Morris-Commercial Leader 3-ton motive units coupled to two streamlined semi-trailers with Brockhouse chassis and Duple bodywork built to the maximum permitted dimensions in 1937 of 33ft. long and 7ft. 6in. wide. These vehicles could accept and send telegrams, service being from the central office serving window with other postal facilities being sold from the other two windows - two telephone booths were situated in the rear of the trailer accessed from the rear door. Like the special airmail van, streamlined styling of the period was used and special fairings were fitted to the motive unit to match the trailers. They attended important open-air functions, such as exhibitions and sports meetings and during the war they were used as Mobile Radio Stations in camouflage livery. The motive units lasted until 1957 but the trailers were still fit for service and they were paired with new Seddons carrying the same registrations. The post-war GPO 2 is featured on page 41 after it was restored by the Post Office but sadly the 1937 trailer was destroyed recently in a motorway accident. (GPO)

Above: Small vans in the rural areas were and still are based singly at village post offices often only visiting the main office for servicing. Keeping the vehicle clean would be the responsibility of the driver and meant getting out the bucket and cloth. The driver would also need to top up the oil in the engine and see to other day to day essentials. This Morris Minor of 35cf. capacity was based at Langton Green in the Tunbridge Wells Head Office area. Note the concrete K3 telephone kiosk. (GPO)

ROYAL MAIL

Surviving the War

The outbreak of the Second World War caused considerable difficulties for the Royal Mail fleet. The last of a long line of Morris Minor mailvans was a batch of fifty delivered in 1940, and the first of the series Z mailvans featured a 50cf. version of the standard coachbuilt body grafted on to the Morris front end, but very soon the factory-built panel van had to be accepted by the GPO. The Morris series Y also joined the fleet for the first time in 1940, again initial deliveries had coachbuilt bodywork by Duple or Simpson & Slater, but by 1941 the GPO was forced to buy standard factory-built steel bodies.

Defence of the Realm certificates were issued in 1940, due to the threat of invasion. These gave exemption from road-fund licences when Road Fund licensing certificates were introduced, a system which applied to GPO mailvans until nationalisation in October 1969. The system was changed in January 1951 and the exemption certificates were known as Crown Ownership numbers.

July 1942 saw the acquisition of 40 second-hand BSA motor cycles from the War Department; they are thought to have been requisitioned machines and were used on telegram delivery work in large cities. The motor cycle combination for mail delivery, which the GPO was well on its way to eliminating in favour of Morris Minor, had also to be bought and 99 were delivered in 1940/41. Fords were also purchased in small numbers including a batch of 100 Ford E83Ws in 1941/2.

The end of the war in 1945 saw deliveries of Morris and Morris-Commercial vehicles in large numbers but coachbuilt bodies did not return to small vans – factory built bodies were now the norm for the two smallest sizes of mailvan. The famous GPO registration mark, which had been transferred to the London County Council, specifically for issue to the Post Office, was used on mailvans in 1946/47.

The first BSA Bantam motor cycles were bought in December 1948 and this machine was to remain the standard telegram bike right through until 1970/71 when the last 400 were bought.

Right: This pre-war Morris-Commercial LC 25/30cwt. chassis was obtained in 1943 and was fitted with an experimental body. Note the masked headlights and the white bumper as required by the blackout regulations. (GPO)

Left: During the Second World War a shortage of petrol meant that many vehicles were modified to run on gas. The gas was usually stored in a bag on the roof of the vehicle requiring a refill each day. The Morris series Z in this photograph dates from July 1940, being of the early examples having the traditional coachbuilt body grafted onto the streamlined front end; it lasted until May 1950 when it was broken up by the GPO. Note the George VI cypher. (GPO)

Right: Another feature of the war was a need to take whatever vehicles were available. 1941 saw the purchase of 100 Ford E83W 100cf. vans. Again blackout measures are clearly visible as is the wheelarch mounted fire extinguisher. Two vehicles from this batch GGY 279 and GGY 280 were later used by the Nigerian Government. (GPO)

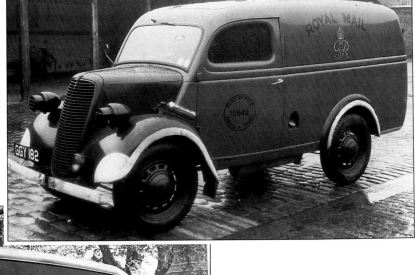

Left: As well as the 100cf. Fords, a similar quantity of Ford Thames were purchased, these being of 250cf. capacity. They were fitted with GPO-pattern tail boards modified rear doors and rubber buffers after delivery. (GPO)

ROYAL MAIL

Above: The GPO was forced to purchase more motor cycle combinations but these were larger BSA 500cc machines. GLO 967 was new in September 1942 at East Grinstead but lasted only until August 1945; most of the wartime deliveries had a similar short life with the GPO. (GPO)

Above: 120 BSA telegraph delivery machines went into service in 1941. This particular machine was a 350cc version purchased under a Ministry of Supply contract. (GPO)

Below: Work at railway stations often meant moving large quantities of mail. Often single or rakes of trolleys needed to be moved and to do this tractors were used. These might be powered by batteries, petrol or liquid petroleum gas.

GLP 838 is a Lister petrol Auto Truck originally numbered PT34 and dates from 1941, it is pictured here towing a wooden barrow of the type still to be found in use today. (GPO)

Above: Scammell Mechanical Horses were developed as railway delivery vehicles but seven were purchased between 1936 and 1941 for postal work moving mail between post offices and railway stations. They were usually to be seen attached to 500cf. trailers. GUV 292 was a three-ton MH3 that operated at Aberdeen. Note the new design of allocation roundel, introduced during the war, very unusually positioned on the offside of the vehicle. (GPO)

Below: The wartime years prevented vehicles receiving their regular overhauls and as a consequence became very scruffy and run-down in appearance. The immediate post-war years saw a gradual return to former maintenance standards – GLO 281 and GXK 388 from 1941 and 1943 meet at Yeading central repair depot – the former was considered beyond repair and was broken up for spares. Standard factory-built bodywork was fitted to most Morris series Z mailvans. (GPO)

ROYAL MAIL

Above: Seen at Euston station is one of two Planet C tractors dating from 1945, it is towing an early example of the All-Steel turntable trailer used in stations singly or in rakes. (GPO)

Above: 1945 saw the introduction of the Morris-Commercial LCS 200cf. GYW 67 had an experimental factory-built body described as unit construction, later classified as 240cf. It was allocated to North Western District Office in London. (GPO)

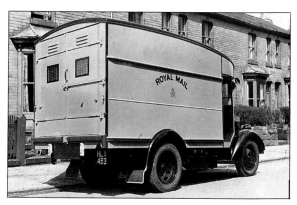

Above: The Morris Y 100cf. van was first used for postal work in 1939 when two were purchased. By the time GYW 973 was introduced into service in 1945 there were 2200 such vehicles. It was photographed on Dulwich Common and worked for Royal Mail from May 1946 to August 1960 – a tribute to both the design and the GPO's maintenance system. (GPO)

Above: HLA 453 was the prototype Morris CV9 360cf. introduced in 1947. It was subsequently re-registered GPO 11 and was the first in a batch of 400 CV9s with Stewart & Ardern bodywork. Vehicles with GPO registrations had to be re-registered prior to sale by Royal Mail and it became 991 BYY in February 1961. (GPO)

Right: In 1946 history repeated itself and the Ministry of Supply disposed of large numbers of war-surplus vehicles and the Post Office acquired some of these. Among them were 11 Bedford OY motive units and HLA 378 is seen here towing one of the mobile post office trailers. (GPO)

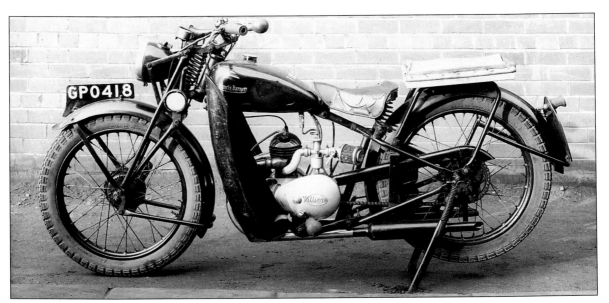

In 1947, nineteen lightweight motorcycles were purchased to evaluate their suitability for telegram delivery. Among them were GPO 418 which was a Francis Barnett Merlin 125cc, HLA 991 an Excelsior Super 98cc Autobyk and a Brockhouse Corgi 98cc lightweight JYU 269 – a folding design developed for use by paratroops, which lasted only twelve months in GPO service from August 1949. The autocycles were a little more successful – GPO 418 was re-registered LUU 993 on sale in April 1951, the same month that HLA 991 was sold. (GPO)

Post-War GPO Years

At the beginning of the 1950s, the GPO was well on its way to recovery from the war years. Mailvans had now settled down to four sizes, all of Morris or Morris-Commercial manufacture. The smallest size, 50cf., remained the domain of the Morris Series Z van until 1953 when the first of the Issigonis designed Morris Minors entered the Royal Mail fleet. This type remained the standard small mailvan throughout the 1950s and 1960s, although fifty Morris Minivans were bought in 1960 and again in 1963, while rather larger numbers of Ford Anglias were purchased in 1964, 1966 and 1967.

The next size of mailvan was rated at 100cf. and the standard choice was the bonneted Morris Y which was superseded by the flat-fronted Morris J in 1950 and the later Morris J4 in 1961. This last model being re-rated at the higher capacity of 150cf. Deliveries of the Morris J4 continued through to its replacement in the British Leyland range at the end of 1973, while the larger 250JU was tried in 1968 and two batches of Bedford CAs was purchased for trials in 1964/5.

The other two sizes still featured coachbuilt bodywork to GPO designs and were rated at 240cf. and 360cf. The smaller version was based on the Morris-Commercial LC3 chassis in 1950, and progressed through LC4 and LC5 versions and eventually using the Morris LD chassis with standard Morris bodywork from 1957. This type was purchased through to 1968 and the first Morris EAs with underfloor engines were purchased by the GPO in the autumn of 1969. The period started with the Morris CV9 chassis being purchased for the larger 360cf., the NVS chassis was bought from 1952, the KNC from 1955 and the LD chassis was the choice from 1958 through to 1970 with coachbuilt bodywork from a number of bodybuilders.

There was a noticeable increase in the number of other types – the Land Rover joined the Royal Mail fleet in 1951 for use in difficult terrain, a batch of Karrier Gamecocks began the use of large mailvans in 1956 with 600cf. bodies and the experiments with parcel concentration resulted in more artics. based on Morris FF, Laird and FJ chassis in the 1960s.

Right: Where small amounts of mail have to be moved around stations or safety prohibits the use of driver ridden trucks, pedestrian controlled electric versions are used. This Lewis example from 1950 is seen at Guildford. (GPO)

The GPO was always ready to test other types of vehicle, the Austin Gipsy rivalled the Land Rover for a while, while single examples of the Standard 7cwt. and 15cwt. vans, Austin A35, Commer Cob, Ford Thames 10/12 cwt. van and early Ford Transit were tried out as mailvans.

The GPO registration letters were used again in 1963 with numbers preceding the letter and in 1965 with the year suffix 'C'. In both cases, telephone vehicles predominated in the issue of registrations, although 200 Morris Minor mailvans and 50 of the trial Bedford CAs made up part of the 1965 allocation.

Left: KGO 989 is a driver ridden version of the electric truck made by Scott. This photograph is taken at Plymouth where it worked until 1967 and then moved to Bath where it lasted until 1970. These vehicles were replaced by Wessex electric tractors of the type illustrated later in this book. (GPO)

Below left: NXO 861, a Morris Minor 50cf. of 1953 was one of the first to be used for postal work. These vans were to become the standard small vehicle with the last being taken into service in 1972. Early examples featured a split windscreen, rubber front wings and high position headlamps. (GPO)

Opposite page:
Top left: Where rough terrain and hostile weather conditions prevail, use is made of four wheel drive vehicles. NYH 496 was one of a second batch of Land Rovers introduced new in September 1954 and it was one of two introduced at Eskdalemuir for Head Postmaster Lockerbie in September 1954. It is a Series One 86 inch wheelbase 60cf. version and lasted in service until November 1966. (GPO)

Top right: Several vehicles of the Seddon marque had been purchased by the Post Office for stores work in 1952 and 1954 and in the latter year three 240cf. Seddon 25 diesels were purchased for postal work. (GPO)

Middle left and right: Perkins engines of Peterborough developed their P3 diesel engine in the early '50s. The engine was incorporated into the Trojan chassis to make a very popular small van. The Post Office in order to evaluate the diesel engines purchased five vans, three of which were the 150cf. and two being of the 240cf. version. (GPO)

Bottom: A third Mobile Post Office was required in 1961 and a standard Morris FF motive unit was used with registration GPO 3. This view shows the unit at Bagshot for the 350th Anniversary celebrations. (M.W.Skillen)

Top: To replace the Mechanical Horse, Scammell introduced the Scarab which had the same three wheel configuration. Probably the largest user was British Railways but the Post Office also took several small batches over the years. 998 CLB is a 1961 3-ton version used to tow 500cf. trailers at Bradford. (GPO)

Left: In the early '60s the Post Office started to make much more use of road transport especially to move parcels. One notable scheme was the East Anglian Road Service which removed all parcel traffic from Liverpool Street station in London with the network based on an office at Canning Town in east London which was later to become the site of the East London Parcel Concentration Office. For such schemes motive units and trailers were required and one such combination of a Morris FF and 1300cf. dropframe trailer is seen here. (GPO)

Above: A single Land Rover 88" petrol mailvan was purchased in 1963. 646 GPO is photographed outside Kirkhill Post Office in August 1972. (A.J.Taylor)

Above: The famous GPO registration mark was issued again in 1965 and among the lucky recipients was a batch of fifty Bedford CA 150cf. mailvans purchased early in 1965 as an extended trial against the BMC J4 design. A rather battered GPO 925C is photographed towards the end of its life in Euclid Street, Dundee in July 1970. (R.P.Doig)

Below: The use of cars in GPO days was generally limited to large saloons for official use by senior managers, although there were exceptions including the purchase of two Ford Anglia cars in plain black, bought in 1965 for more general use in South Wales.

The first of these two cars was GUC 813C photographed outside its Newport base in November 1979 still looking very smart despite its age. The use of pressed aluminium number-plates was unusual on GPO vehicles. (M.D.Street)

Above: In 1957 the Morris LD02 360cf. was introduced. It was to remain the standard large van until the Leyland EA came out in 1971. By the time NYV 651E, which was the first to have a plywood body, came into service in 1967 1740 LDO2s had been purchased by Royal Mail. A further 430 were to enter service in the next four years. (GPO)

Left: Ford Anglias were tried as mailvans in 1964 with a batch of a thousand vans. In 1966 and 1967, both Morris Minors and Ford Anglias were purchased in similar numbers and one of the 1967 deliveries was NMH 377E photographed in Brighton in May 1972. The white R on the front indicates that the vehicle is used as a Reserve to cover for other vehicles, a ratio of one reserve to six vehicles being the norm. Greater reliability of modern vehicles and easier servicing requirements has reduced the reserve cover very considerably. (R.P.Doig)

Above: Superseding the Morris JB was the later Morris J4 design which was bought with both petrol and diesel engines. Illustrated is one of the large 1965 delivery photographed early in 1966 at Battersea when nearly new and before the allocation lettering had been added to the roundel. Roof-mounted registration plates were fitted to these vans in the mid-1960s but later ones had them attached above the front bumper. The last J4s were delivered to the Post Office in 1974. (D.J.Foster)

Left: NYY 999E was an interesting vehicle based on the London FX4 taxi. It was an Austin of 200cf. capacity and it was bought to appraise its tight turning circle. No more were purchased after it was found to be unstable when fully loaded. The application of the allocation roundel to the offside door was very unusual. (GPO)

Right: The smaller Morris LD 240cf. was purchased until 1968. One of the later deliveries, SYF 729F, new in 1967, is photographed in Cardiff in the late-1980s. It survived long enough to be renumbered 7166759 in the 1974 re-numbering and received the 1976 'Double-line' bilingual lettering style, although larger lettering would have been an improvement. (M.J.O'Sullivan)

Top: Another purpose-built Mobile Post Office unit was purchased in 1969, a Karrier Gamecock tender coupled to a caravan-style Mobile Post Office trailer. The combination is photographed at Sophia Gardens, Cardiff. (M.D.Street)

Bottom Left: Sixteen Scammell Townsman mechanical horses were purchased in 1967 and a further eighteen followed in 1968. This photograph shows one of the latter batch, SYF 932F, in Glasgow in July 1968 and coupled to the inevitable 500cf. semi-trailer. (R.P.Doig)

Bottom right: The last GPO registration series allocated to Royal Mail was AMD-H but this was only partly used in the last two months of the GPO's existance. Among the vehicles in this registration were a batch of BMC Laird LR1800 motive units which replaced the Morris FFs on the East Anglia parcels scheme. Two from this batch, AMD 351/3H, are pictured at Westwood Parcels Office in Peterborough in April 1970. (A.J.Taylor)

Royal Mail in Colour

Top left: Some horse-drawn contractors mailvans were still in use before the second world war – this particular example which has survived into preservation, is thought to have been a McNamara vehicle. (M.W.Skillen)

Top right: The replica of the McNamara Dennis built by the Post Office at Kidbrooke in 1969 and pictured here at Quorn station on the Great Central Railway during a Royal Mail event. (M.W.Skillen)

Middle: A view of mobile post office GPO 2, coupled this time with the 1957 Seddon motive unit which had a Perkins P6 engine, David Brown gearbox and Eaton two-speed rear axle. The location is Quorn station on the Great Central Railway. (M.W.Skillen)

Left: A rare example of a Morris Y with coachbuilt bodywork by Simpson & Slater survived in private ownership long enough to be repurchased by the Post Office in 1985 and restored to its original 1940 mailvan livery. This vehicle is now part of the National Postal Museum's Heritage Vehicle Collection.

Top left: Another vehicle from the Heritage Fleet is this 1956 Morris KNC 360cf., again fully restored by the Post Office to original condition. This view at Arley in May 1990 shows it on one of its first outings after restoration. (M.W.Skillen)

Top right: A 1960s fibreglass-bodied mailcart photographed at Porthmadog in July 1988. (D.Worth)

Left: A privately preserved mailvan is this 1966 Morris Minor mailvan JLW 576D photographed at the Horsham Historics rally. (M.W.Skillen)

Below: Illustrating the light blue livery used by Television Licence vehicles is this standard Morris Minor mailvan used on these duties in Cardiff. (M.D.Street)

Left: The red and white livery used on Postal Engineering was a familiar sight on small and medium vans from 1971 until the mid-1980s, but it was rare on large vans; shown here is a 1976 Leyland 420EA mailvan used as a stores van in South Wales. (M.D.Street)

Middle: The Post Office Management College at Coton House at Rugby bought this Bedford VAS5 with Plaxton Supreme 29-seat coachwork for transport to and from the college. It is photographed at Reading Mechanised Letter Office in June 1989. (D.A.Cott)

Bottom: Efforts to publicise the use of postcodes led to a number of vehicles being painted in a special silver postcodes livery in the early 1980s. Most major centres in the North-East had a vehicle in the special livery but other locations including Oxford had similarly liveried vehicles. This view shows a 1980 Leyland 345EA 240cf. and 1981 Sherpa 150cf. from the Head Postmaster Darlington fleet. (North Eastern Postal Board)

Top left: This Bagshot view of Land Rover LAX 847X illustrates both the 350th Anniversary logo in colour and the Welsh bilingual livery. This particular van was one of a number of Land Rovers based at Abergavenny for deliveries into the Black Mountains. (M.W.Skillen)

Middle left: In the 1980s, the Royal Mail logo was strengthened in prominence with larger lettering and with the addition of Postcode, Datapost or Parcels lettering. Parcels lettering was added to larger vehicles irrespective of their actual use. This view shows a 1985 Leyland Roadrunner 8.10 with Besco 600cf. bodywork which operated on parcels duties at Portsmouth until 1987 when it moved to Brighton for letters work. (M.W.Skillen)

Middle right: A 1984 Ford Cargo postal engineering van was converted to a long-wheelbase transporter at Royal Mail's Bamber Bridge depot in 1990/91 and is pictured in 1992 at Preston carrying a new Sherpa 400 workshop van and a preserved Bedford HA van. (M.W.Skillen)

Right: An unique colour scheme was the finishing of a standard semi-trailer as a parcel by the Eastern Postal Region. The 1982 Leyland Chieftain motive unit was unusual in being registered by Leyland before delivery to the Eastern Postal Region at Milton Keynes in June 1983. (M.D.Street)

Top right: Support services have led a colourful existence over the last 30 years. Originally these were supplied by the telephone service but from 1968 a separate postal engineering function was set up by the GPO and a number of telephone vehicles were repainted from green to red. In 1971 the livery was brightened up with a white waistband which was changed to yellow in the early 1980s. In 1989, these services were reorganised into a new division of the Post Office offering building engineering contracting and consultancy services known as RoMEC. A distinctive grey-white livery was introduced and existing vehicles were repainted including this 1983 Ford Transit van photographed in Norwich in March 1989. (R.W.Taylor)

Top left: A Renault cash carrier at Reading MLO in April 1989 illustrates the late eighties livery of these vehicles. (M.W.Skillen)

Top right: Among the vehicles to receive the 1990 Parcelforce livery was this 1986 Ford Escort based at the Parcel Depot at Winnersh, near Reading and photographed outside Hungerford Post Office in July 1990. (D.A.Cott)

Middle: Parcels vehicles continued to be delivered with Royal Mail lettering in 1987-1989 prior to the launch of the Parcelforce livery early in 1990. Vehicle purchasing policy was much less conservative and more imported vehicles were acquired. 1988 arrivals included 10 Mercedes-Benz Powerliner artics and five MAN 17-292 motive units with sleeper cabs, one of which is featured in the photograph. Based at Peterborough with local number 218, it is pictured at Mountergate Parcels Office, Norwich where it is coupled to a 1987 semi-trailer of 2250cf. capacity allocated to Leeds.

Left: In addition to the standard Royal Mail cruciform introduced in 1990, a special variant was produced for vehicles used on International Letters work. The result is illustrated on G214 UKR, a Leyland-DAF Freighter 17.18 seen at Dover, fitted with Besco 1400cf. bodywork and a type which has been purchased in small numbers in recent years where a larger rigid vehicle was required. (M.W.Skillen)

Top Left: Despite the formation of RoMEC, some engineering vehicles continued to be required for maintenance duties. Standard vans were adapted for engineering duties at the Post Office depot at Bamber Bridge, near Preston and this view shows a Leyland-DAF 200, one of 57 similar vehicles bought in 1990/91, 26 in RoMEC livery. This particular van was registered H792 WAO and worked at Carlisle. (M.W.Skillen)

Top right: The white and dark blue colour scheme first used on the 1981 Sherpas was retained for the next generation of television detectors bought in 1989/90. Twenty-two of these Leyland-DAF 400s were converted at Kidbrooke with some equipment transferred from the 1981 vehicles, these vans now form the current detector fleet. (M.W.Skillen)

Left: RoMEC has also bought estate cars in recent years and these are white rather than light grey giving a rather brighter and smarter livery. This 1991 Ford Escort estate J370 XHK was photographed at its Newcastle base. (D.A.Cott)

Left: Illustrating the 1990 Parcelforce livery on a standard Leyland-DAF 400-series parcels van is this view of H656 BSP at Dundee. The application of the lettering tends to be variable and vehicles often do not have the gold Royal Mail lettering and occasionally the gold cyphers on the cab doors. (D.M.Hinde)

Opposite page – bottom left: Parcelforce introduced a Gold Depot Award Scheme in 1991, aiming to measure customer service at each of its then 174 depts. Each quarter a winning depot was picked from each operational area and a number of vehicles were repainted in a special gold livery for allocation to a winning depot for the next quarter. A Leyland-DAF Roadrunner is photographed inside Norwich depot in May 1992; the wheeltrims, fairings and wind deflectors were special fitments on the gold vehicles. (R.W.Taylor)

Left: The majority of vehicles operated by Post Office Counters are anonymous cars but this vehicle carries the full livery of the organisation. This Ford Transit van H470 NNO, new in 1991, was photographed in January 1992 at Dunstable. (R.W.Taylor)

Middle: In 1991, Royal Mail's discounted service was branded STREAMLINE and a large batch of motive units and trailers were delivered that year with special Streamline lettering. This view shows one of 38 Leyland-DAF 95.360Ati 38-tonne artics bought in 1991 and paired with a tri-axle trailer from the Cardiff depot. (J.P.Targett)

Bottom right: A white livery has been adopted by Quadrant, the Post Office's Catering Services. This Leyland-DAF 400 van is photographed at Basingstoke in January 1995. (P.J.Rogers)

Left: In October 1990, the first Royal Mail green vehicle was shown at the International Motor Show in Birmingham, it combining generally available environmentally friendly features in one truck. Since then a range of Concept Vehicles has been developed, all finished in a special Royal Mail green livery. Illustrated here is the largest of the green fleet, a Leyland-DAF FTG95-360 with a low-noise 364 bhp engine, road speed limiter, air suspension, electronic tyre pressure monitor, catalytic exhaust and in-cab rear-view monitor. The trailer, by Cartwright, has an air-operated rear shutter, Ricardo aerodynamic styling with skirts, energy absorbing rear bumper, air suspension, automatic weighing device on each axle, Hope anti-jack-knife and spray suppression kit. (J.P.Targett)

Middle right: Purchasing & Logistics Services based at Swindon has adopted a bright green livery. Illustrating this livery is a Schmidt 2016 Streetking road sweeper bought new in February 1995. (P.J.Rogers)

Middle left: The current Parcelforce artic livery is illustrated with this view of Peterborough-based Leyland-DAF 80.300Ati K227 AEG paired with a Manchester-based trailer at Norwich. (D.A.Cott)

Left: Leyland-DAF 400 K621 XPD stands outside the yard of Banbury delivery office in November 1994. This particular van has not long returned from supporting a sponsored bike ride from Lands End to John o'Groats. (P.J.Rogers)

Post Office Corporation 1969 – 1981

The General Post Office ceased to exist in October 1969 and a new state-owned organisation known as The Post Office Corporation took its place. It is probably true to say that the change went unnoticed by the majority of citizens and Royal Mail is still widely referred to as the GPO over 25 years later. The change in vehicle purchasing policy was slight and the Post Office continued to buy Morris Minors, J4s and LDs as long as they were available.

The demise of the Morris Minor in 1971 caused particular problems for Royal Mail as there appeared to be no satisfactory replacement. Fifty Reliant three-wheelers were tried in 1970 and had a predictably short existence of less than three years and the Post Office had little option but to buy the BLMC Minivan in 1972-1974. These proved to be unpopular with mechanics and drivers alike, on the grounds of lightweight construction and low build. The Morris Marina was also tried in 1973-1974 but between 1975 and 1978, Royal Mail favoured the Bedford HA, the van derivative of the Vauxhall Viva. The years 1979-1983 saw the purchase of the Marina van again or the Ital derivative and this type was later uprated to 80cf.

The medium size van saw considerable change in the 1970s. British Leyland's J4 design was bought until the end of its production in 1973, then the Commer Spacevan was favoured in 1974 and again in 1976. The new Leyland Sherpa design was purchased in 1975 while Dodge Spacevans were bought in both 1977 and 1978. Thereafter the Leyland Sherpa returned to favour from 1979 and continues to be purchased in 1995, although Freight-Rover, Leyland-DAF and LDV badges have replaced the Leyland badge over the years. In larger sizes, the BMC EA van was first bought in GPO days and it was the standard large mailvan for much of the 1969-1981 period, the Post Office being the majority user of the later deliveries.

The expansion and diversification of the fleet continued in this period with large numbers of motive units being purchased in the 1970s of Ford, Bedford, Dodge and Leyland manufacture. The increasing mechanisation of mail-handling resulted in the purchase of large numbers of various types of wheeled containers, together with fork-lifts, pallet trucks and electric tractors. Postbuses, which had been introduced experimentally in GPO days, expanded considerably in the 1970s and settled down to purchases of Commer (and later Dodge) Spacevans converted for postbus work. Scotland found this size of bus too big for many routes and instead used estate cars or Land Rovers on routes requiring a lower seating capacity.

Below: Wessex was favoured with a large batch of thirty-five electric tractors bought in the autumn of 1969. They were used for work at various stations and included five to renew the Bath fleet; one of the five is pictured crossing from station to the sorting office with a single turntable trailer in tow. (M.J. O'Sullivan)

Below: Raleigh mopeds were bought in the 1967 to 1970 period for use on both telegram delivery and letter work. Those for letters tended to be used in flat, rural areas such as Lincolnshire where they were well suited. Those for telegram work enabled the Post Office to reduce the age of the delivery boy which helped in recruiting suitable staff for this work. This particular example is a Raleigh Runabout RM6 machine used at Hull. (M.W. Skillen)

Top left: By 1970, it was clear that the Morris Minor had no future in plans of British Leyland and a replacement small mailvan would soon be needed by the Post Office. Bedford HAs and Ford Escorts had both been tried, and two batches of Morris Minivans had been operated without much success. It was decided to try a batch of Reliant Supervan III three-wheelers as a possible alternative. A batch of fifty was supplied in late 1970 and they entered service in comparison with Morris Minors. One of the trial locations was Tamworth, where two are photographed outside the delivery office in September 1971. Driver reaction to the trial was not positive and after one burnt out in service at Warrington in 1973, the entire batch of fifty was withdrawn and sold. (A.J.Taylor)

Top right: Sixty Leyland 700FGs with Cravens 600cf. bodywork were purchased in the autumn of 1970. They were the first general purchase of this chassis for mailvan use, although the GPO and the Post Office had purchased large numbers for the telephone fleet from 1959. They were not a success in many Royal Mail fleets and those delivered to Central London were quickly banished to the provinces. This Glasgow-based vehicle, AGD 626J, is photographed outside Kyle of Lochalsh Post Office in April 1973. This particular vehicle later worked at Edinburgh and survived until April 1980. (A.J.Taylor)

Middle left: Another large Scottish mailvan is UFS 633J of Glasgow photographed in May 1972. The BMC EA 240cf. was introduced just before the demise of the GPO and the first 250 were badged as BMCs. The next batch, bought in 1970, carried Austin-Morris badges while those delivered in 1973 were badged as Leylands. (R.P.Doig)

Left: Cravens bodywork was again specified for most of the 1971 delivery of 600cf. mailvans but the choice of chassis was the Bedford TK. This view shows one of the batch still in service at Guildford in March 1980 and still carrying the traditional 1953 lettering style. The addition of ROYAL MAIL across the front of the vehicle at this time was very unusual, although common-place in the 1950s. It was later reintroduced in 1984. Reflective registration-plates were adopted as standard by the Post Office in June 1971. (M.J.O'Sullivan)

Left: The last batch of Morris Minors was a delivery of 2001 in 1971/72. Not all were used as mailvans and this one has been adapted as a dual-control driver-trainer with Wales & The Marches Postal Board. Note the rooflight which allows fresh air to the rear seat where the instructor is housed. (M.D.Street)

Below: Postbuses have become quite a common sight in certain parts of the country but are usually based on the minibus. The Post Office had a few much larger personnel carriers usually for internal work and this vehicle started life at the Post Office Management College near Rugby where it was used to ferry students to and from Rugby station. The vehicle was registered FNX 580K and was subsequently transferred to the Western Isles where it performed Postbus duties. It was a Leyland Terrier 750TR with a Lex-SMB body with 24 seats, although on its conversion to a PSV it lost some of its seats. (The Post Office)

Above: With the demise of the Morris Minor the Post Office had to seek a replacement. The BLMC Minivan was chosen but was not particularly popular in some offices as staff found the restricted headroom a problem when on delivery work. In country areas their low ground clearance was also a problem with underbody damage being common. Many were used for telegraph delivery work and as Inspectors vehicles on patrol work. This particular vehicle had an additional separate roof-mounted mail compartment. (GPO)

Left: British Leyland suspended production of the EA in 1972 to permit the transfer of production from Adderley Park to Washwood Heath. The 1972 requirement for medium vans was met instead by 110 Commer KCBN4023 chassis which were fitted with bodywork built at the Bamber Bridge depot made up of Glasonite panels with a Wideslat sliding rear shutter and rated at 400cf. The end-product was quite a pleasing vehicle. Motor auctions were used to dispose of old vehicles from the 1960s and the sight of vehicles devoid of lettering awaiting sale at commercial vehicle auctions remains a common sight – the first of the batch was photographed awaiting sale at Tower Bridge Auctions in London in January 1982. (C.M.Hogan)

Right: Containerisation of the mails was begun at the end of the 1960's and in 1972 twenty-one Leyland Terrier TR650s with Imperial bodywork and tail-lifts were bought as a trial. They were designed solely for container transport and this view of a Birmingham vehicle clearly shows containers (known as POTUs – Post Office Trailers Universal) stowed in the front of the lorry. Not surprisingly, the design proved to be too restrictive and they were quickly converted to conventional 600cf. mailvans. (M.D.Street)

Below: The Commer 2500 design was tried in 1967 but the BMC J4 design continued to be the standard 150cf. mailvan. The end of J4 production before the launch of the new Sherpa model allowed Commer to get a foothold with Royal Mail, and the 1974 delivery was for 710 vans of the PBRM2000 type. Photographed in December 1981 in Sutton, Surrey is one of the 1974 delivery, it being in the company of a similar Dodge PBRM2090S from 1978. The 1974 vehicle has been repainted and relettered in the 1975 livery. (C.M.Hogan)

Left: A variety of Leyland, Dodge and Ford motive units, operating at 20-22 tons gcw, were purchased in the 1970s for medium-distance trunking of parcels and letters. Seventy-five Dodge K2011Ps were purchased in 1974 and several were allocated to Reigate & Redhill for trunking work in Kent, Surrey and Sussex centred on a new concentration depot at Salfords, near Horley. This June 1983 view shows the unit at Salfords. (M.W.Skillen)

Right: Successor to the J4 in the BL range was the Sherpa. The Post Office ordered, early in 1974, 325 examples of the new design known as the BL215. The first vehicles did not arrive until the spring of 1975 and carried the traditional gilt livery. A further 550 followed on from the first order badged for the first time as the Sherpa. The photograph shows 5080217 from the first batch carrying the special bilingual Welsh livery introduced for the Prince of Wales' Investiture at Caernarvon in 1969 and was taken in Cardiff in 1978. (M.J.O'Sullivan)

Left: The Sherpa van was often retained after its normal 7/8 year life as a mailvan as a workshop runabout. This one worked for Birmingham at West Bromwich until 1981, it then became a workshop vehicle at Hockley with extra lights and a yellow band. (M.W.Skillen)

Above: Guy Big Js were used by the telephone supplies fleet of the Post Office from 1967 but their use was not extended to the Royal Mail fleet until 1972 when five were supplied for trunking work from east London to the Channel Ports. Twenty-two more, for general work, were bought in 1975. This view shows one of two from the batch that operated initially at Peterborough and later moved to Birmingham. The circular allocation roundel device disappeared with the revised 1975 livery and vehicle allocations were then shown in plain black lettering on the nearside cab door. This May 1984 view shows the unit at the Midland regional depot at Stratford-upon-Avon, by now it had been relegated to car-transporter and yard-shunting work. (M.D.Street)

Left: Cars were preferred to vans from 1976 for driver-instruction work when a large delivery of forty-three Vauxhall Viva 1300L saloons was received. Finished in plain red, only the registration and the special 'L-plates' used by the Post Office gave any clue to the their Post Office ownership. PCD 6R operated for the South Eastern Postal Region and is photographed in spring 1983; the special learner plate having been neatly covered up when not in use. (M.W.Skillen)

Left: The BSA Bantam was not available after 1971 and the Post Office bought the Austrian-built Steyr-Daimler Puch MV50 moped for a mixture of postal and predominantly telegram delivery work from 1972 to 1979. The early deliveries of these two-speed mopeds were equipped with a standard pedal start while the final order in 1979 for 650 machines found a conventional kick start in favour. Two from the 1976 order, part of Brighton's fleet at that time of sixteen mopeds, are photographed at the side of the Head Post Office in Brighton (M.W.Skillen)

Below: Expresspost was introduced in 1978 as a new premium-rate delivery service, in most cases using small mailvans for the delivery work. In two cities, Bristol and Oxford, delivery work was undertaken by four Honda CD175 motor cycles at each location. They were the first motor-cycles, as opposed to mopeds, purchased by the Post Office since the last BSA Bantams arrived in 1971. One of the Oxford machines is photographed inside the local workshop in May 1982. Note the tyre-pressure, a feature of mailvans since the war, neatly applied above the exhaust. (M.J.O'Sullivan)

ROYAL MAIL

Left: WUL 19S started life as a standard Leyland 345EA 240cf. mailvan used on International Telegrams work, one of a batch of 302 similar vehicles bought in 1977. Under the separation of British Telecom from the Post Office in 1981, the van passed to BT along with overseas telegraph operations. This May 1983 view shows the van outside Electra House in London, having exchanged its red livery for the BT yellow with blue lettering. (M.W.Skillen)

Right: Bedford HAs were bought from 1975 to 1978 as the standard small mailvan. This view shows one of the 1978 delivery photographed at Londonderry in Northern Ireland and carrying the neat double-line lettering introduced for these vans in 1975. Northern Ireland was unusual in that all vans were registered in Belfast, rather than by the local Head Postmasters. The Bedfords had no provision for posters and they had to be stuck on the bodywork as it evident on this van with the remnants of one still present. (Motorphoto)

Left: The Dodge Spacevan 2090P was the standard choice for postbus in the late 1970s when considerable expansion of the number of services operated by the Post Office took place. Not all were Dodges and the 1979 delivery of 107 postbuses included five Ford Transits with Dormobile 12-seat conversions to PSV standards. One of the five is pictured on the Dunoon-Tighnabruich service shortly after delivery. (Motorphoto)

Left: Most of the motive units bought in 1979 were Ford Ds made up of 14 D1110s, 26 D2014s and 10 D2114s. Representative of the D2014s is KNJ 519W photographed at Salfords Parcel Depot in June 1983. With the reorganisation of the Post Office in October 1986, this unit passed to South East Parcels. (M.W.Skillen)

Below: Royal Mail turned to the Leyland Marathon for maximum-weight artics in 1978. In addition to a number purchased by the Post Office, these two units were on extended hire at Cardiff and received full Royal Mail livery. (M.D.Street)

The Eighties and Nineties

The Post Office turned to Ford in a big way from 1984 when the first Ford Escort mailvans were purchased; the following year's deliveries standardised on diesel engines for the first time to give Royal Mail an all-diesel fleet by the end of the 1980s. Other types have been tried in this period including Ford Fiestas, Vauxhall Astramaxes, Vauxhall Combos and Ford Couriers. Medium-sized mailvans have generally favoured the Sherpa design with large numbers of the wide-bodied variant purchased from 1984.

Parcelforce was set up on its own in 1986 and soon adopted a separate vehicle purchasing policy. Its standard delivery van has been based on the Sherpa design but larger vehicles of AWD, Iveco, Mercedes-Benz, VW, Ford and Leyland-DAF manufacture have joined its fleet in recent years. All transport of parcels was switched to the roads during the 1980s and a large fleet of trunking units has been built up using higher-specification trucks than those favoured in the earlier decade.

Mechanisation of the mail, its concentration on a smaller number of sorting centres and a policy to use air and road transport over long-distances and short-distances respectively has reduced Royal Mail reliance on the railways. This decade has seen the pace of change accelerate with heavy investment in new Processing Centres and with a new pattern of rail operation expected to start shortly with the commissioning of new Royal Mail trains and a new facility at Willesden in north London for their operation.

In 1990, Royal Mail changed its livery to one based upon the cruciform logo with the double line yellow stripes. This livery change coupled with a policy of replacing small vans after only three years, has resulted in a much smarter fleet in the 1990s than for several decades previously. Thus re-reinforcing the general public's perception of the little red van – the common link in the network which delivers mail to many millions of addresses in the United Kingdom every working day.

Below: The last vehicles bought by the Post Office for telegram delivery were 25 BL Minivans purchased in 1981. When telegram delivery ceased in October 1982, this van was still in store at Falkirk and it was not registered until January 1984 when it was used as a conventional mailvan, being ousted by a Ford

Escort in 1990 and then finding further work at Alloa where it was photographed in the summer of 1990. In recent years, the age of small mailvans has been progressively reduced from 6 years to 3 years to give a modern fleet and to get the best financial payback from replaced vehicles. (P.Walton)

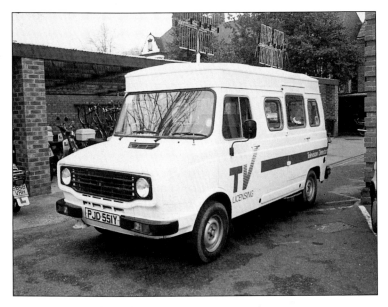

Left: Some of the best known Post Office vehicles are the Television Detectors housing sophisticated equipment to detect unlicensed reception of television programmes. In GPO days estate cars were used, followed by a delivery in 1968 of special Commer 2500 Spacevans with automatic transmissions registered SGW 750F to SGW 761F and finished in a light-blue livery. Further similar vehicles were bought by the Post Office in 1970 and 1977. The fleet was all but worn out by 1981 when twenty-two Freight Rover Sherpas were bought as replacements. These Sherpas have 1.7 petrol engines and manual transmission and a host of special equipment including a heavy duty alternator and two 100 amp batteries, Alpinair air-conditioning equipment, a high-roof modification and extended side and rear doors. The interior fittings and electronics were supplied by Kenure Developments. Although purchased in 1981, they did not enter service until the autumn of 1983 and introduced a new white livery with blue waistband and lettering. This view shows one of the batch in Norwich in January 1989. (R.W.Taylor)

Right: The Post Office tried Ford Transits and Bedford CFs again in 1981, and fitted them with fibreglass high-roof extensions by Walkers of Watford. Fifty of each were purchased and this Brighton view in July 1985 illustrates one of the Bedfords. (M.W.Skillen)

Below: After the Bedford HAs purchased in 1975-1979, the Post Office reverted to British Leyland and purchased Morris Marinas in 1979-1982. Initially classified as standard 50cf. mailvans, the type was later uprated to a capacity of 80 cubic feet. The Marina was restyled and updated in 1982 and the later deliveries were badged as the Ital. This view shows one of the Marinas at Grantown-on-Spey. (M.W.Skillen)

Opposite top: Another Lorry Driver of the Year final finds a 1982 Dodge 100-series G2011P motive unit with a standard semi-trailer. (M.D.Street)

Opposite bottom: This May 1990 view shows two publicity vehicles operated by the Post Office. On the left is a Ford Transit which has both a demountable luton body and flat body depending on requirements and on the right is a standard Leyland Chieftain motive unit KJR 49X which initially worked from the parcels concentration office at Washington, Co. Durham but later found further use on publicity work. The semi-trailer to which it is coupled dates from the late 1960s and both have been smartly repainted in a red and yellow livery. (M.W.Skillen)

Above: The Post Office was again tempted with smaller mailvans in 1983 and the Austin Metro and Ford Fiesta were both tried. The photograph shows the two prototypes at Stratford-on-Avon in May 1983. The Metrovan worked at Thurnby for Head Postmaster Leicester and was joined by 427 more in 1983 and 620 in 1984. The Ford Fiesta demonstrator entered service at Bury St. Edmunds and was joined by 50 further vans later in 1983 and 100 diesel-engined vans in 1984. They had quite short lives in Post Office service. (M.W.Skillen)

Above: The Post Office celebrated the 350 years since King Charles I first opened up the Royal Mail for the public in 1635 with a number of events culminating in a special ceremony at Bagshot which was attended by the Prince of Wales. A 350th Anniversary device was produced for the celebrations which was affixed to a large number of vehicles in 1985. Pictured here is a 1984 Leyland Terrier 600cf. at Bagshot in this livery. (M.W.Skillen)

Left: Kawasaki motor cycles found favour in the mid-1980s and this view shows one of the twenty-four Kawasaki 250S Scorpions bought in 1985. The entire batch was based at East Central District Office in the City of London for Expresspost and Datapost deliveries. (M.W.Skillen)

ROYAL MAIL

Above: 1984 was a watershed for small mailvans with Austin Metros, Austin Maestros, Ford Escorts and Ford Fiestas. The Ford Fiestas and 100 of the Ford Escorts had diesel engines and this type of engine was adopted as standard for 1985 and subsequent orders. Just 70 of the newly introduced Austin Maestro van were purchased in 1984 but the type did not find favour with Royal Mail. This van, photographed at the 350th Anniversary Celebrations at Bagshot, was based in the City of London where vans carried the inscription The Postmaster Controller EC District Office rather than the standard Head Postmaster lettering. Just visible is a 1985 Kawasaki Datapost motor cycle. (M.W.Skillen)

Left: Mailcars are used quite extensively for postal deliveries in other European countries especially France. Royal Mail bought two small batches of Ford Fiestas and Ford Escorts in 1983, a much larger delivery of 600 Fiestas in 1985 and another eighty Ford Escorts in 1987 but the van has proved to be the 'best buy' for most work. Fiesta diesel mailcar C78 JAK was photographed at Hope, Derbyshire in 1989 shortly before replacement by a conventional Escort van. (M.W.Skillen)

Top: Electric Bedford CF C649 MYJ carries Princes Charles away from the 350th Anniversary Celebrations at Bagshot, as an example of the latest in mailvan technology it contrasts with the horse-drawn mailcoach in which he arrived at the 1985 event (M.W.Skillen)

Middle: Another major trial of battery-electric propulsion took place in 1984 with 80 vehicles divided between Bedford CFs and Freight-Rover Sherpas. This view shows one of the Sherpas outside the Head Post Office in Brighton in the same location as the 1905 view of a Thomas Tilling mailvan. Note the heavier wheels and the underslung batteries visible below the open cab door. Brighton's hills proved too much for the electrics and they had to be shadowed by conventional diesel vans because of frequent breakdowns and this particular example later moved westwards along the coast to Portsmouth. (M.W.Skillen)

Left: The Ford Escort diesel mailvan was first purchased in quantity in 1985 and has thereafter remained the standard small mailvan. The 1985 delivery of 2,904 is represented by C651 MYJ brand new at the Bagshot celebration. One of this batch was supplied to St. Helena and was in still in use in 1994. (M.W.Skillen)

Above: The investment by the Post Office in larger, more efficient premises often meant that these were located on the outskirts of town and cities with an eye to easy access to local motorways. One effect of this move away from city centres has been the need to obtain more personnel carriers to transport staff to and from their duties. Ford Transits were favoured in 1983-1985 and this view shows one of the 1984 batch of ten vehicles when new; this one later entered service at Reading at the new parcels office at Winnersh. (M.W.Skillen)

Left: Another Bagshot view is this Freight-Rover Sherpa 320cf. registered specially for the event. Freight-Rover introduced the wide-bodied Sherpa in 1983 and this vehicle quickly became a firm favourite with the Post Office for both letters and parcels work. (M.W.Skillen)

Above: The Pedestrian Electric Delivery Truck is a type unique to the Post Office, consisting of a large box body with a central shelf and sliding doors on both sides, mounted on four-wheeled chassis of the type used for street sweepers' carts. Some 483 were bought by the Post Office between 1954 and 1970, the majority replacing handcarts on parcels delivery. The first new trucks for many years were 102 bought in 1986 made up of sixty Harbilt to the traditional design and illustrated by D682 KKH photographed at Beverley in June 1991. (R.W.Taylor)

Middle: In addition to the sixty Harbilts bought in 1986, a further forty-two were purchased from Wingrove and Rogers Ltd. of Kirkby with a modern angular body incorporating a full-width shutter on the nearside – a big improvement on the sliding doors that only give access to half the body at a time. This view shows D867 UDY, itself somewhat unusual in having a former Hastings mark issued by Brighton registration office, at Burgess Hill shortly after delivery. P.E.D.Ts. have found a variety of uses including for children's rides at carnivals, as a mobile pillar box based at Tonbridge to ease pressure on pillar boxes and several have become Postman Pat vans in recent years as illustrated later in this book (M.W.Skillen)

Left: A third type of electric truck is the ride-on truck with bodywork for mail carriage. These were familiar sights at places such as Leeds, Doncaster, Lincoln and Norwich. Illustrated is one of four Electricars LP2/24s delivered to Norwich in 1986 and photographed at the Norwich Open Day in May 1988. Electricars, a new company based at Atherstone, has been successful in recent years in gaining several orders from the Post Office. (R.W.Taylor)

Above: The Post Office originally obtained two Suzuki mailvans in 1985 for use on the Scilly Isles. Two Bedford Rascals were demonstrated the following year and this resulted in the purchase of 35 Rascals plus the two demonstrators. Illustrated is D923 HUC from this delivery at the 1987 Lorry Driver of the Year final and which subsequently worked at Ascot. Another batch of thirty-five Rascals followed in November 1987 and these were tried in a number of areas but the use of this type of vehicle is now restricted to Cornwall and the Isles of Scilly. Next to the Rascal is the long-wheelbase wide-bodied Sherpa, carrying false numberplates with BPO representing British Post Office; this size was rated at 400cf. for mailvan work. (M.W.Skillen)

Middle: Eighteen Electricars C5000 battery-electric Tow-Tractors were purchased in 1986 for station work and the first of the batch is pictured at Reading mechanised letter office in June 1989. The five at Reading did not initially carry any registrations but this one was later registered Q272 YRX for use on public highways. (D.A.Cott)

Right: This Sherpa 150cf. was new at Guildford but was used for livery experiments at Bamber Bridge in connection with the new lettering style introduced in 1990 with the Royal Mail 'cruciform' logo. Note the rear shutters that were specified by some fleets as an alternative to the standard hinged door. (M.W.Skillen)

Above: The Parcels business was more adventurous in its purchasing policy after its formation in 1986; three experimental batches of ten artics bought in 1987 were ERF E10s, Seddon-Atkinson T17L25s and ten Renaults but the main deliveries were Leyland Roadtrains and Ford Cargos. Illustrating the Ford Cargo CA2824 28-tonne artic is D137 ETP which operated at Southampton for Royal Mail Parcels. (M.W.Skillen)

Left: Small batches of Ford Transits have been bought by the Post Office from 1973 for mailvan work. Sixty were purchased in 1987 and this view shows E164 FCD when new at Brighton. This was one of 30 350cf. mailvans fitted with side-doors for evaluation. (M.W.Skillen)

Above: The wide-bodied Sherpa was also used as a postbus from 1984. The first few deliveries had proprietary conversions but soon the work was being done at the Post Office's own depot at Bamber Bridge. Illustrated is one of twenty 1987 conversions. E964 PWY was new at Ripon for the Masham service but later moved to Newtown as a reserve for the New Mills service. It is photographed at Arley in May 1990 when it was used to transport visitors from the Severn Valley Railway station to the show site used by the Post Office for a Family Fun day. (M.W.Skillen)

Left: Pictured here in May 1990 at North Walsham is one of the 1987 batch of Escort diesel mailcars. (R.W.Taylor)

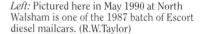

Left: Land Rovers have continued to be used in difficult locations and this 1987 Land Rover 90 was allocated to Saxmundham as a replacement for a 1975 Land Rover which then found further use as the Lowestoft workshop recovery vehicle. The new Land Rover was photographed shortly after delivery in July 1988. (D.A.Cott)

Left: One of sixteen Seddon-Atkinson 3-11 Turbo motive units purchased by Royal Mail in 1987 and photographed here in June 1988 outside Bournemouth sorting office coupled to a 1981 40' semi-trailer. (C.F.Martin)

Middle left: Royal Mail Parcels bought 880 Ford Cargos in 1987/88 and fitted them with 1000cf. bodies in order to set up a second tier of parcels deliveries for Heavy and Large Consignments which did not fit into the more mechanised standard parcels operation. The operation was termed Network Two by the Post Office but survived only a few years after which the two parcels operations were integrated together again. One of this large delivery, E161 FAP with Besco bodywork, is photographed in Eastbourne after it received the 1990 Parcelforce lettering. (L.N.Simpson)

Bottom left: Second-hand vehicles were rarely used by Royal Mail but when a batch of fifty Freight-Rover Sherpa 300s became available in September 1988, the Post Office was tempted to take them on lease. The fifty were part of a batch of 178 that formed the bulk of Newsflow, an NFC subsidiary set up in 1987 to distribute the Mirror Group's London newspaper, the London Daily News. They were supplied and registered by Arlington Motors of Willesden. The London Daily News ceased publication and the fifty were taken on twelve months hire after which it is believed they were purchased by the Post Office. D649 BLL illustrated here at Norwich in February 1989 became part of the Post Office's Internal Fleet Hire based in Kidbrooke in south east London. (R.W.Taylor)

Above: Although the Sherpa was the standard medium van, several batches of Ford Transits were operated by Royal Mail. F756 KMA was part of a small batch of such vans that operated at Cardiff in full Welsh bilingual livery. (M.W.Skillen)

Right: Parcelforce has had a number of attempts to use the demountable concept in its vehicle fleet, and in 1988 it purchased five Leyland Roadrunner 8.13 chassis and ten Ray Smith bodies of 850cf. capacity. The photograph shows one of these combinations doing a delivery run in Exeter in June 1989 – no doubt leaving the nearside roller shutter door unattended is not encouraged by Parcelforce management. This vehicle was delivered during the transition period before the launch of the new Parcelforce identity early in 1990. (M.D.Street)

Left: Cashco is the Post Office's cash-carrying operation, and in recent years specialised vehicles have been bought specifically for this work. Illustrated is one of the 1987 Freight-Rover Sherpa 310s converted by Johnsons Engineering at Toddington and new to London but it had moved to Exeter by the time the photograph was taken in June 1993. (B.Jenkins)

Below: Royal Mail Parcels continued its more adventurous vehicle-purchasing in the late 1980s with medium-sized vans. 1989 deliveries included sixty VW LT50s with Vaile & Co. (Dorset) luton bodywork as illustrated by G138 CJT based at Bournemouth for 'Heavy & Large Consignment' delivery work. It was photographed at Bridport in June 1992. (B.C.Read)

Below: Originally a Pedestrian Electric Delivery Truck built by Manulectric in 1967, PMG 814E was refurbished in the early 1980s as a Postman Pat van for shows such as a Fun Day organised by the Post Office staff newspaper Courier at Arley in May 1990. The registration letters PMG are thought to have been allocated to the GPO because of their association with Postmaster General who was a Cabinet Minister in charge of the GPO. (M.W.Skillen)

Opposite top: Mercedes were also favoured by Parcels and sixteen 609D integral panel vans were among the 1988 order. This April 1989 view at Norwich shows the newly delivered and unlettered van which was later registered F43 CAH. (R.W.Taylor)

Opposite bottom: Twenty-seven Iveco Daily 49.10 vans also arrived in 1989 and this 1990 view shows the new Parcelforce lettering to advantage. (K.Porter)

Top: Ten years of postbuses. This photograph taken at Leyburn in August 1990 shows a 1989 Leyland-DAF 14-seat Sherpa G290 JBV alongside preserved 1980 Dodge postbus B449 GUF owned by one of the Post Office Vehicle Club's members. (D.A.Cott)

Above: Personnel Carriers started to be used in greater numbers from about 1983 for the transport of postmen to and from new delivery offices. From 1987, the use of these vehicles was taken one step further and they were used as a means to efficiently transport postmen out to their walks. A number of different types of vans have been developed to allow bicycles to be transported or to be used as conventional 150cf. mailvans. They are known within Royal Mail as Postmen Accelerators and many hundreds are now in service with the Post Office. A typical recent example is J224 KBJ, a wide-bodied Leyland-DAF 400, based at Great Yarmouth but photographed visiting Norwich in February 1992. (R.W.Taylor)

Right: Slightly less usual is this diesel tractor, one of two used to tow trailers at Derby between the station and the nearby sorting office. In recent years, Derby has become a key centre for interchange between road, rail and air in Royal Mail's quest to improve the standard of service of provincial mail. (M.W.Skillen)

Above: The Leyland Sherpa has been the standard 150cf. mailvan from 1979 but it has been the subject of many facelifts and rebadgings during its twenty years of production. Two such vans are pictured at Sunderland sorting office in March 1992; on the right is a 1988 Freight-Rover Sherpa and on the left is a 1991 Leyland-DAF 200 van. The older van carries a local Newcastle registration while following a restructuring in 1992, new vehicles were registered at nine Divisional Offices in England and Scotland with Northern Ireland continuing to register its vehicles at Belfast. (D.A.Cott)

Below: A revised Ford Escort, known as the Mk V, was introduced in 1991. A large delivery of 4419 such vehicles arrived in 1991 and included H615 GRT located to Woodbridge and photographed at its base shortly after delivery in May 1991. (R.W.Taylor)

Above: Another view of two postbuses, one in preservation. The current choice for estate-car postbuses is the Peugeot 405 and this view shows J979 VSG at Selkirk in May 1992, having been delivered the previous month fitted with a special sumpguard to protect the engine in country lanes. Next to it is preserved Ford Sierra A971 LSH, one of twenty-seven 1600 estate cars, which also operated from Selkirk. (D.A.Cott)

Below: The Post Office was disappointed by the number of niggling faults with the 1991 Ford Escorts and turned to Vauxhall as an alternative supplier for its small van. 1991 deliveries favoured Ford but 1992 purchases favoured Vauxhall and this resulted in the two types entering service simultane-ously. This view on 1st August 1992 shows Ford Escort K82 XEG destined for Harleston next to Vauxhall Astramax K81 XEG destined for Wymondham. The Vauxhall Astramax proved to be no more reliable than the Ford Escort in the arduous daily service of Royal Mail and vehicle orders continue to be divided between the two manufacturers. (D.A.Cott)

Above: Bamber Bridge depot is the location for this view of an Iveco-Ford Cargo 0813 with its Post Office assembled 600cf. bodywork having the finishing touches applied; registered H866 JBM by Ford, this vehicle was used at Cardiff with its RSG cantilever tail-lift. (M.W. Skillen)

Above: Royal Mail's presence at railway stations will diminish in the next few years. This 1992 view at Glasgow Central shows the traditional trainside delivery to a passenger train which is soon to disappear. (D.A.Cott)

Right: Cashco has also purchased Mercedes-Benz vehicles in recent years including this 1992 814D with another Johnsons conversion. This location for this August 1993 is Selkirk and the van appears to have both English and Scottish cyphers displayed on the bodywork. (D.A.Cott)

Left: Eighteen Land Rover postbuses were bought in 1992 including two long-wheelbase models, one of which is K408 BSG. It is based at Blairgowrie and was photographed en-route to Glenshee. (D.A.Cott)

Above: Grangemouth workshop deals with accident repairs for Royal Mail vans throughout Scotland. Purchased specially for this work is this Leyland-DAF slideback recovery vehicle whose platform 'slides back' at an angle and reaches the ground, obviating the need for ramps. In addition, the vehicle has an extending suspended tow mechanism. This August 1994 view shows the vehicle loaded up with Escorts L335 MFS and L338 MFS at its base. (P.D.Robinson)

Below: Another hundred Ford Transits were bought by Royal Mail in 1992, among them South Kensington based L130 GYE photographed in October 1994. (D.A.Cott)

Right: Parcelforce developed a 530cf. collection and delivery van based on the Leyland-DAF 400 chassis and fitted with lightweight bodywork derived from Cartwright's Parcelpacker; the body uses lightweight Carbofont composite panels and has an electrically operated nearside door. This July 1994 views show a Cardiff-based van. (M.D.Street)

Right: After the Astramax went out of production, Royal Mail bought the Vauxhall Combo as the alternative small van. Over a thousand such vans have been purchased in 1994/95 and this view shows M579 KPF outside Banbury workshop just before entering service in February 1995. (P.J.Rogers)

Left: The offshore islands of Jersey, Guernsey and the Isle of Man were all part of the GPO operation until October 1969. Each island then set up its own postal administration; the vehicle illustrated is a 1994 LDV 200 mailvan in the latest Jersey livery which reverts to plain red, having adopted a red and yellow colour scheme immediately after the separation from the British Post Office. Jersey's cypher device incorporates the Plantagenet Crown over a Post Horn, the latter symbol used by many continental administrations. (L.N.Simpson)

Left: Rebodying of Royal Mail vehicles has taken place at times over the years but rechassising of vehicles was without precedent until 1995 when continued warranty problems with some 1992 Iveco Cargo chassis led to their replacement with later 1995 75E15 chassis. One of the first chassis exchanges took place on this Wolverhampton-based example whose body has been refitted to a new chassis registered by Progress Trucks, an Iveco dealer. The paintwork of the body contrasts sharply with the gleaming chassis. (P.J.Rogers)

This book is the work of the Post Office Vehicle Club, an enthusiast society dedicated to all aspects of road transport operation by the GPO, and its successors the Post Office and British Telecom.

The Club was formed to bring together people interested in current operations and vehicle purchases, and this interest remains to this day. In addition, it encourages the preservation of Royal Mail vehicles and a large number of preserved vehicles are owned by members of the Club. The Post Office has made over a significant amount of historic data on GPO vehicles and this information is being incorporated in the Club's historic records.

For more information on the Post Office Vehicle Club, please contact the Secretary at the address below.

POST OFFICE VEHICLE CLUB
7 Bignal Rand Drive, Wells, Somerset. BA5 2EU.

The Largest single collection of preserved Royal Mail vehicles is the Post Office's own Heritage Vehicle Fleet, now under the care of the National Postal Museum having been transferred in 1994 from Royal Mail Transport Services at Kidbrooke. This fine collection now numbers over fifty vehicles. These date from the early 1930s through to more modern times giving a broad representation of the varied role road transport has played within the Royal Mail structure over the years.

At present this collection is stored in Gloucestershire and, unfortunately, public access is not currently possible. In the long term, the National Postal Museum is working towards housing the Heritage Vehicle Fleet in larger and more accessible premises where it will be on view to the general public demonstrating the vital role these vehicles have played over the years.

NATIONAL POSTAL MUSEUM
King Edward Street, LONDON, EC1A 1LP.